Sniffy

Claire Llewellyn
Illustrated by Mike Gordon

RIGBY

Nina and Chimp were playing at home.
Dad came in with a box.
Dad said, "Come and see what is in the box."

Nina looked in the box.
There was a puppy!

The puppy sniffed Nina.
He sniffed Dad.
He sniffed Chimp.
Then he sniffed Nina again!

Nina said, "I don't like him.
He sniffs too much."
Dad said, "He's just a puppy.
Let's call him Sniffy."

The next day, Nina and Chimp were playing
on the bed.
Sniffy wanted to play too.

Sniffy jumped on the bed.
He sniffed Nina.
He sniffed Chimp.
Then he sniffed Nina again!

Nina said, "I still don't like him.
He sniffs too much.
Tell him to go away!"
Dad said, "But Nina, he's just a puppy."

The next day, Nina and Dad went to the park.
They took Chimp and Sniffy.
Nina and Chimp were playing on the swings.
Sniffy wanted to play too.

Sniffy ran round and round the swings.

He sniffed Nina.

He sniffed Chimp.

Then he sniffed Nina again!

Nina said, "I still don't like Sniffy.
He sniffs too much and gets in the way."
Dad said, "He's just a puppy.
He only wants to play."

The next day, Nina was playing at home.
She wanted Chimp, but she could not find
him anywhere!
Nina looked and looked for Chimp.

Sniffy wanted to look too.

He sniffed the bed.

He sniffed the box.

But he could not find Chimp.

Dad said, "Let's go to the park.
Let's see if we can find Chimp there."

Dad and Nina looked for Chimp at the park.
But they could not find Chimp.

Sniffy wanted to look too.
First he sniffed Nina.
Next he sniffed the swing.
Then he sniffed Chimp!

Nina said, "Dad, Sniffy's just a puppy, but I like him!"